AF879290

Revocation of a Power of Attorney Kit

EstateBee

By EstateBee Publishing

Bibliographic Data

- International Standard Book Number (ISBN): 978-1-913889-11-1
- Printed in the United States of America
- First Edition: December 2010
- Second Edition: January 2014
- Third Edition: September 2020

Published By: EstateBee Limited,
23 Lynn Road,
London SW12 9LB,
United Kingdom

Printed and Distributed By: Kindle Direct Publishing, an Amazon Company

For more information, e-mail books@estate-bee.com.

Copyright

"Revocation of a Power of Attorney Kit" is © EstateBee Limited 2020. All rights reserved. No part of this kit may be reproduced, stored in a retrieval system, or transmitted by any means – electronic, mechanical, photocopying, recording, or otherwise – without the prior consent of EstateBee.

Trademarks

All terms mentioned in this kit that are known to be trademarks or service marks have been appropriately capitalized. Use of a term in this kit should not be regarded as affecting the validity of any trademark or service mark.

Warning and Disclaimer

Although precautions have been taken in preparing this kit, neither the publisher nor the author assumes any responsibility for errors or omissions. No warranty of fitness is implied, and all implied warranties are excluded to the fullest extent permitted by law. The information is provided on an "as is" basis. Neither the author nor the publisher shall be liable or responsible to any person or entity for any loss or damages (whether arising by negligence or otherwise) arising from the use of or reliance on the information contained in this kit or from the use of any forms or documents accompanying it.

Important Note

This kit is meant as a general guide to revoking a power of attorney. While effort has been made to make this kit as accurate as possible, laws and their interpretation are constantly changing. As such, you are advised to update this information with your own research and/or counsel and to consult with your personal legal, financial, and/or medical advisors before acting on any information contained in this kit.

The purpose of this kit is to educate and entertain. It is not meant to provide legal, financial, or medical advice or to create any attorney-client or other advisory relationship. The authors and publisher shall have neither liability (whether in negligence or otherwise) nor responsibility to any person or entity with respect to any loss or damage caused or alleged to be caused directly or indirectly by the information contained in this kit or the use of that information.

About EstateBee

EstateBee, the international self-help legal publisher, was founded in 2000 by lawyers from one of the most prestigious international law firms in the World.

Our aim was simple - to provide access to quality legal information and products at an affordable price.

Our will writing software was first published in that year and, following its adaptation to cater for the legal systems of various countries worldwide, quickly drew more than 40,000 visitors per month to our website. From this humble start, EstateBee has quickly grown to become a leading international estate planning and asset protection self-help publisher with legal titles in the United States, Canada, the United Kingdom, Australia, and Ireland.

Our publications provide customers with the confidence and knowledge to help them deal with everyday estate planning issues such as the preparation of a last will and testament, a living trust, a power of attorney, administering an estate and much more.

By providing customers with much needed information and forms, we enable them to place themselves in a position where they can protect both themselves and their families using easy to read legal documents and forward planning techniques.

The Future....

We are always seeking to expand and improve the products and services we offer. However, to do this, we need to hear from interested authors and to receive feedback from our customers.

If something isn't clear to you in one of our publications, please let us know and we'll try to make it clearer in the next edition. If you can't find the answer you want and have a suggestion for an addition to our range, we'll happily look at that too.

Using Self-Help Kits

Before using a self-help kit, you need to carefully consider the advantages and disadvantages of doing so – particularly where the subject matter is of a legal or tax related nature.

In writing our self-help kits, we try to provide readers with an overview of the laws in a specific area, as well as some sample documents. While this overview is often general in nature, it provides a good starting point for those wishing to carry out a more detailed review of a topic.

However, unlike an attorney advising a client, we cannot cover every conceivable eventuality that might affect our readers. Within the intended scope of this kit, we can only cover the principal areas in each topic, and even where we cover these areas, we can still only do so to a moderate extent. To do otherwise would result in the writing of a textbook which would be capable of use by legal professionals. This is not what we do.

We try to present useful information and documents that can be used by an average reader with little or no legal knowledge. While our sample documents can be used in most cases, everybody's personal circumstances are different. As such, they may not be suitable for everyone. You may have personal circumstances which might impact the effectiveness of these documents or even your desire to use them. The reality is that without engaging an attorney to review your personal circumstances, this risk will always exist. It's for this very reason that you need to consider whether the cost of using a do-it-yourself legal document outweighs the risk that there may be something special about your particular circumstances which might not be taken into account by the sample documents attached to this kit (or indeed any other sample documents).

It goes without saying (we hope) that if you are in any doubt as to whether the documents in this kit are suitable for use in your particular circumstances, you should contact a suitably qualified attorney for advice before using them. Remember the decision to use these documents is yours.

We are not advising you in any respect.

In using this kit, you should also consider the fact that this kit has been written with the purpose of providing a general overview of the laws in the United States. As such, it does not attempt to cover all the various procedural nuances and specific requirements that may apply from state to state - although we do point some of these out along the way. Rather, in our kit, we try to provide forms which give a fair example of the type of forms which are commonly used in most states. Nevertheless, it remains possible that your state may have specific requirements which have not been taken into account in our forms.

Another thing that you should remember is that the law changes - thousands of new laws are brought into force every day and, by the same token, thousands are repealed or amended every day. As such, it is possible that while you are reading this kit, the law might well have been changed. We hope it hasn't, but the chance does exist. To address this, when we become aware of them, we do send updates to our customers about material changes to the law. We also ensure that our books are reviewed and revised regularly to take account of these changes.

Anyway, assuming that all the above is acceptable to you, let's move on to exploring the topic at hand.........revoking a power of attorney.

Table of Contents

Revocation of a Power of Attorney

What is a Power of Attorney?

A power of attorney (also referred to as a "POA") is a legal document by which you can appoint and authorize another person (usually a trusted friend, family member, colleague or adviser) to act on your behalf and to legally bind you in that respect. While most people fail to see the importance of having a power of attorney, there are many compelling reasons why they should be used.

For example, suppose that:

- you are going to be out of the country for an extended period and need someone trustworthy to manage your business affairs while you're away; or
- you wish to acquire real estate in another state, and you need to authorize a local to sign and lodge documents on your behalf; or
- you want someone to manage your real estate for you; or
- you're getting a little bit older and wish to appoint someone you know and trust to make healthcare decisions on your behalf should the day come when you are unable to do so yourself.

A power of attorney can be used to facilitate your needs in each of these scenarios.

The person giving the power of attorney is usually referred to as the 'donor', 'grantor' or 'principal', while the recipient is called the 'agent', 'attorney-in-fact' or just plain 'attorney' (which doesn't mean they have to be a legal practitioner).

Types of Powers of Attorney

There are several different types of power of attorney that you can make. Each of these serve a different set of needs and requirements. Some of the main types of power of attorney are detailed below.

General Power of Attorney

A 'general power of attorney' is virtually unlimited in scope. It allows your agent to act as your authorized legal representative in relation to the whole cross-section of your legal and financial affairs, until such time as that authorization is terminated. In other words, your agent will have full legal authority to make decisions and take actions on your behalf, as if you were taking them yourself. This could, for example, include signing letters and checks, executing contracts, opening and closing bank accounts, and so on.

While you cannot generally limit the scope of the power conferred under a general power of attorney, there are nonetheless some presumed limits to the agent's authority. For example, your agent is not normally permitted to assume any position or office that you might hold. These offices would include positions as employee, company director, trustee, personal representative, and others. In addition to that, your agent cannot execute a will on your behalf (or amend an existing one), take action concerning your marriage or delegate his or her authorization under your power of attorney to a third party, unless expressly authorized to do so in the power of attorney document. An agent is also prevented from making gifts of your assets, other than small gifts that you yourself might have been expected to make having regard to the size of your estate.

A general power of attorney (unless stated to be durable) automatically comes to an end if you become mentally incapacitated or die. It will also come to an end on any termination date set out in the document itself.

General Power of Attorney Kit

For more information on general powers of attorney, check out our General Power of Attorney Kit.

Get your copy at
www.estate-bee.com/product/general-power-of-attorney-kit/

Limited Power of Attorney

A 'limited power of attorney' is like a general power of attorney except that it imposes specific and sometimes substantial limits upon the authorization granted to your agent. This could, for example, be a limit to the scope or duration of the authority granted to your agent.

Often, people granting powers of attorney limit their agent's authority to completing specific transactions or tasks. For example, you may appoint someone as your agent solely for the purpose of having them sign a document on your behalf but only in a format pre-approved by you and attached to the power of attorney document itself. Alternatively, you can appoint your agent for the sole purpose of dealing with a single task or transaction (such as the sale of a piece of real estate to a specified individual at a specified price and on specified terms). These types of limitations remove a substantial part of the risk associated with granting powers of attorney. The good news is that there are no limits on the limitations you can impose on your agent's authority. So, you can be as precise in the authority you grant your agent as you wish.

Limited Power of Attorney Kit

For more information on limited powers of attorney, check out our Limited Power of Attorney Kit.

Get your copy at

www.estate-bee.com/product/limited-power-of-attorney-kit/

Like the position with a general power of attorney, you will remain personally liable for the actions of your agent.

The limited power of attorney will continue in force until it comes to an end on a date set out in the power of attorney document – assuming there is one. In any event, it will automatically come to an end if you become mentally incapacitated or die.

Healthcare Power of Attorney

One of the most common forms of power of attorney in use today is the 'medical' or 'healthcare' power of attorney.

A healthcare power of attorney allows you to authorize an agent to make healthcare decisions on your behalf if you are incapacitated and unable to make those decisions yourself. The authorization conferred on your agent can cover any form of healthcare decision. Unlike documents such as living wills, the agent's authority under a healthcare power of attorney can apply even where you are not terminally ill or permanently unconscious. So, for example, it could apply if you suffered temporary unconsciousness (if you were in an accident, for instance) or if you were suffering from a mental illness like Alzheimer's disease which affects the decision-making process.

Unlike general and limited powers of attorney, a healthcare power of attorney does not automatically terminate if you become incapacitated. Better still, you can even specify in your healthcare power of attorney document that your agent's authority only comes into effect if your physicians determine that you have become incapacitated or are otherwise unable to make decisions for yourself.

In your healthcare power of attorney document, you can specify guidelines and directions regarding the types of medical treatment you wish to receive during any periods in which you are unable to make healthcare decisions on your own behalf. Other than in the most extreme cases, your agent will be obliged to follow these instructions and direct your physicians to follow them. As an alternative to expressly specifying your wishes, you can also give your agent full discretion to make healthcare decisions on your behalf during any period in which you are unable to. Of course, be mindful who you give such authority to.

Healthcare Power of Attorney & Living Will Kit

For more information on general powers of attorney, check out our Healthcare Power of Attorney & Living Will Kit.

Get your copy at

www.estate-bee.com/product/healthcare-power-of-attorney-living-will-kit/

Ordinary and Durable Powers of Attorney

In addition to the three types of powers of attorney that we have just described, powers of attorney can also be categorized as either being 'ordinary' or 'durable'.

Ordinary powers of attorney are only valid for as long as you can make decisions on your own behalf. If you die, or become mentally incapacitated, your power of attorney immediately ceases to have effect and your agent's authority immediately comes to an end. If this happens, your family and business partners could be left in a situation where they are powerless to legally deal with your affairs without seeking court intervention. Some examples of typical problems include the inability to transfer real estate held in joint names, deal with bank accounts that require dual signatories, and the execution of legal documents generally.

Durable powers of attorney, on the other hand, remain valid even if you become mentally incapacitated. In fact, under many durable powers of attorney, your agent's authority to act only becomes effective if you become incapacitated. By giving a trusted family member, friend, or adviser authority to legally make decisions on your behalf while incapacitated, you can ensure that your family's interests and business interests are protected. Of course, like all powers of attorney, durable powers of attorney will come to an end if you die.

Durable Powers of Attorney

For more information on durable powers of attorney, check out our durable power of attorney kits.

Get your copy at **www.estate-bee.com/product/durable-general-power-of-attorney/**

Get your copy at **www.estate-bee.com/product/durable-limited-power-of-attorney-kit/**

In a durable power of attorney that only becomes effective if you become incapacitated, it is usual to see a clause which provides that a doctor must personally examine you and determine that you are incapacitated and unable to handle your financial affairs before your agent's authority will come into effect. It is that determination that then acts as the trigger for your agent's authority to commence.

To be recognized as durable, your power of attorney must contain a clear and unambiguous statement to the effect that it is intended to be 'durable'. It is also helpful to inclu[illegible]xpress statement to the effect that 'this power of attorney shall not be affected by my [illegible]ent incapacity' or that 'this power of attorney shall become effective upon my incap[illegible]tatements of this type help make it clear that your power of attorney was intended to be du[illegible]nd to be valid even if or after you became incapacitated.

Springing Powers of Attorney

A 'springing' power of attorney is one that becomes effective at a future time or on the occurrence of a future event. That event could include your incapacity or might be something as simple as the date upon which you complete the purchase of a piece of real estate, open a bank account, or otherwise. Springing powers of attorney can be general or limited, as well as ordinary or durable. They can even be healthcare powers of attorney.

Mutual Powers of Attorney

Mutual powers of attorney are usually made between a husband and wife, and occasionally between the members of smaller businesses or professional firms. They serve as indicators of the mutual trust, confidence, and reliance that the parties enjoy within their relationship.

Under these powers of attorney, each spouse or partner will appoint the other (or others) as their agent so as to ensure that their joint plans are implemented in the unfortunate event that one of them is rendered unable to act by illness or injury. For this reason, they are usually durable powers of attorney. As between a husband and wife, they are often durable general powers of attorney (which are unlimited in scope), whereas between business partners they are often durable limited powers of attorney (which, as the name implies, are limited in scope).

Cascading Powers of Attorney

A cascading power of attorney is simply a form of power of attorney which allows for the appointment of alternative or substitute agents. Its purpose is to provide for a backup agent in the event that the first agent named in the power of attorney is unable or unwilling to act, and then provide for further backups to replace the substitute agents if they too decline to act or cannot act for any reason.

What is Revocation?

Revocation is the legal name given to the termination or cancellation of an agreement or instrument (such as a power of attorney). Provided you are not incapacitated, you can revoke your power of attorney at any time by sending a 'notice of revocation' to your agent. This is a written notice signed by or on behalf of a person who granted a power of attorney stating that he or she is terminating the authority conferred on the agent under a power of attorney.

Why Revoke a Power of Attorney?

There are several reasons why you might want to revoke your power of attorney. It may be that:

- your power of attorney is no longer necessary as you can now act on your own behalf.
- you no longer trust your agent.
- you have found a more suitable person to act as your agent.
- it is no longer practical to have your agent acting on your behalf.
- the purpose behind granting your power of attorney has been fulfilled and you no longer need an agent to act on your behalf.

The revocation of a power of attorney is not effective against an agent or any third party who may rely on it until such time as the notice of the revocation has been received by that person. As such, it is common practice to send a written notice of revocation by recorded delivery to the agent and all third parties who may rely on the power of attorney. This then puts them on notice that the agent's authority has been revoked.

Must a Power of Attorney be Revoked in Writing?

Given that the revocation of a power of attorney is not effective against the agent or any third party who may rely on it until such time as notice of the revocation has been received by that party, it is prudent to have a written document evidencing the revocation. This document in turn can be sent (by recorded delivery, if necessary) to all third parties who may rely on the power of attorney to put them on notice that your agent's authority has been revoked.

When Can a Power of Attorney be Revoked?

Provided that you are of sound mind and capacity, you can revoke a power of attorney at any time, regardless of any termination or end date specified in your power of attorney document. However, you will need to be careful when it comes to 'irrevocable' powers of attorney – powers of attorney which are stated to be irrevocable during a specific period. In such cases, a revocation or attempted revocation could be viewed as a breach of contract and could lead to the agent taking legal action against you to preserve the agent's authority under the power of attorney.

How to Revoke a Power of Attorney

To revoke your power of attorney, you must complete the following steps:

- Complete a notice of revocation form (there is a sample at the end of this kit).
- Have your notice of revocation witnessed or acknowledged before a notary public.
- Provide a copy of your executed notice of revocation to your agent and request that he or she returns all his/her copies of the power of attorney to you.
- Provide a copy of your executed notice of revocation to any financial institutions or other third parties who may rely on your power of attorney.
- Provide a copy of your notice of revocation to any agency where your power of attorney has been recorded (e.g. County Clerk's Office, Deeds Registry or Titles Office).

Sample notice of revocation forms have been included at the back of this kit to assist you in revoking an existing power of attorney that you have made. If you have any queries in relation to the procedure or the documents used, or their application to your particular circumstances, it may be advisable to speak to an attorney licensed in your state.

Appendices

Appendix 1

Signing Instructions

Instructions for Completion of The Notice of Revocation of a Power of Attorney

1. Carefully read all the instructions below.
2. Print out the document which you intend using and complete it neatly using a pen or carefully edit the text version of the form (that is available to you to download) on your computer.
3. On the cover page of the document, insert the date of execution of the notice of revocation as well as your name, as principal, in the spaces provided.
4. The first paragraph of the document identifies the parties to the original power of attorney and its date. In this paragraph, you will need to enter (i) your name and address, (ii) the date of the power of attorney and (iii) the name of your agent.
5. Arrange to meet with a notary. Once you meet the notary, you should proceed to step 6 – in the notary's presence.
6. In the execution block, enter the date, month, year, and place of execution. Then sign your name on the signature line above the words "The Principal" in the presence of the notary and two witnesses.

   Your witnesses should not be a person who is:

   - your agent or attorney-in-fact.
   - the notary acknowledging your signature.
   - a relation by blood, marriage, or adoption to you or your agent; or a spouse of any such person.
   - financially responsible for your medical care.
   - entitled to any portion of your estate following your death.
   - a beneficiary under an insurance policy on your life.

- entitled to make claim against your estate (such as creditors).
- your attending physician, nor an employee of such a physician.

7. You should have the two witnesses who witnessed your execution of the notice of revocation complete the "Witness Affidavit" section of the document.
8. You should then have a notary complete the "Notary Affidavit" section of the document.

Note: It is not legally required to have a notary witness the execution of your notice of revocation. So, you can dispense with this step if you wish – although you should still have your signature witnessed by two witnesses. It is, however, good practice to have your notice of revocation notarized as it helps prevent a successful challenge to its authenticity.

Appendix 2

Notice of Revocation of a Power of Attorney

Downloadable Forms

Blank copies of this notice of revocation form can be downloaded from the EstateBee website. Simply login to your account or, if you don't have an account, you can create one for free.

www.estate-bee.com/login

Once logged in, go to your profile page and enter the code listed below in the 'Use Codes' tab:

REVPOAKITNOT698

Notice of Revocation

of

____

(Principal)

Dated this _____ day of ________________, 20____

EstateBee

www.estate-bee.com

Notice of Revocation

I, ______________________________ of ____ ______________________________________ aged eighteen years and upwards hereby revoke, countermand and make null and void my Power of Attorney dated _______________(the "Power of Attorney") and granted in favor of __________________________________(the "Agent", which expression shall include any successor agent appointed under the Power of Attorney) and all rights, powers and authority thereby given to the Agent shall hereby lapse and cease.

Executed this _____________ day of _______________________________, 20 _____, at _____ ____.

____

The Principal

Witness Affidavit

I declare, on the basis of information and belief, that the person who signed or acknowledged this document (the principal) is personally known to me, that he/she signed or acknowledged this Notice of Revocation of a Power of Attorney in my presence, and that he/she appears to be of sound mind and under no duress, fraud, or undue influence. I am not related to the principal by blood, marriage, or adoption, either as a spouse, a lineal ancestor, descendant of the parents of the principal, or spouse of any of them. I am not directly financially responsible for the principal's medical care. I am not entitled to any portion of the principal's estate upon his/her decease, whether under any Will or as an heir by intestate succession, nor am I the beneficiary of an insurance policy on the principal's life, nor do I have a claim against the principal's estate as of this time. I am not the principal's attending physician, nor an employee of the attending physician. No more than one witness is an employee of a health facility in which the principal is a patient. I am not appointed as Healthcare Agent or Successor Healthcare Agent by this document.

Witness No. 1

Signature: ____________________________

Print Name: ____________________________

Address: ____________________________

____

____

____

Telephone: ______________________

Date: ______________________

Witness No. 2

Signature: ______________________

Print Name: ______________________

Address: ______________________

____

____

____

Telephone: ______________________

Date: ______________________

Notary Affidavit

State of ______________________ County of ______________________

_

On this __________ day of __________, 20 ____, before me, ____________________, Notary Public, personally appeared ______________________________, personally known to me (or proved to me on the basis of satisfactory evidence) to be the person whose name is subscribed to the within instrument and acknowledged to me that he/she executed the same in his/her authorized capacity, and that by his/her the signature on the instrument, he/she executed the instrument.

Witness my hand and official seal.

Signature ______________________________

My Commission Expires: ________________

(SEAL)

EstateBee's Online Will Writer

Create Your Estate Planning Documents Online in Minutes...

EstateBee's online software enables you to create bespoke estate planning documents such as wills, living trusts, living wills and powers of attorney from the comfort of your own home.

The software uses documents which have been pre-approved by experienced estate planning lawyers and are tailored to comply with the individual laws of each state (except Louisiana).

Using a simple question and answer process, you'll be able to create a document which is bespoke to your individual circumstances. The process only takes a few minutes and help, and information are available at every step.

Get Started Online Now

Why choose EstateBee's Online Will Writer

- ✔ Save Time and Money
- ✔ Created by Experienced Attorneys
- ✔ Advanced Features
- ✔ Compliant with US Laws
- ✔ Bank Level Encryption
- ✔ 20+ years in Business

Proud to have helped thousands of people make wills, trusts, and powers of attorney online over the past 20 years.

EstateBee's Estate Planning Range

Make Your Own Last Will & Testament

Make Your Own Living Trust & Avoid Probate

Make Your Own Medical & Financial Power of Attorney

How to Probate an Estate - A Step-by-Step Guide for Executors

Estate Planning Essentials - A Step-by-Step Guide to Estate Planning

Funeral Planning Basics – A Step-by-Step Guide to Funeral Planning

Legal Will Kit

Living Trust Kit

Healthcare Power of Attorney & Living Will Kit

Codicil to a Last Will & Testament Kit

Durable General Power of Attorney Kit

Durable Limited Power of Attorney Kit

Made in United States
North Haven, CT
10 November 2026

22097467R00017